Learning to Read, Step by Step!

Ready to Read   **Preschool–Kindergarten**
• big type and easy words • rhyme and rhythm • picture clues
For children who know the alphabet and are eager to begin reading.

Reading with Help   **Preschool–Grade 1**
• basic vocabulary • short sentences • simple stories
For children who recognize familiar words and sound out new words with help.

Reading on Your Own   **Grades 1–3**
• engaging characters • easy-to-follow plots • popular topics
For children who are ready to read on their own.

Reading Paragraphs   **Grades 2–3**
• challenging vocabulary • short paragraphs • exciting stories
For newly independent readers who read simple sentences with confidence.

Ready for Chapters   **Grades 2–4**
• chapters • longer paragraphs • full-color art
For children who want to take the plunge into chapter books but still like colorful pictures.

STEP INTO READING® is designed to give every child a successful reading experience. The grade levels are only guides; children will progress through the steps at their own speed, developing confidence in their reading. The F&P Text Level on the back cover serves as another tool to help you choose the right book for your child.

Remember, a lifetime love of reading starts with a single step!

Thank you to Alex Hastings, Anastasia Suen,
and Jessica Burnham for helping me with the words
and initial designs.

For my late father, Moshe, who bought me
my first camera when I was ten years old,
and for my mother, Tova, the most
supportive person on earth.
—D.S.

Visit us on the Web!
StepIntoReading.com
randomhousekids.com

Educators and librarians, for a variety of teaching tools, visit us at RHTeachersLibrarians.com

Library of Congress Cataloging-in-Publication Data
Names: Salomon, David, author.
Title: Penguins! / by David Salomon.
Description: New York : Random House Books for Young Readers, [2017] |
Series: Step into reading (Step 2)
Identifiers: LCCN 2017001663 (print) | LCCN 2017007935 (ebook) |
ISBN 978-1-5247-1560-1 (paperback) | ISBN 978-1-5247-1561-8 (glb) |
ISBN 978-1-5247-1562-5 (ebk)
Subjects: LCSH: Penguins—Juvenile literature. | BISAC: JUVENILE NONFICTION /
Animals / Marine Life. | JUVENILE NONFICTION / Photography.
Classification: LCC QL696.S473 S25 2017 (print) | LCC QL696.S473 (ebook) | DDC 598.47—dc23

Printed in the United States of America
10 9 8 7 6 5 4 3 2 1

This book has been officially leveled by using the F&P Text Level Gradient™ Leveling System.

STEP INTO READING®

A SCIENCE READER

PENGUINS!

by David Salomon

Random House New York

It is spring in Antarctica.

(Say: ant-ARK-tih-kuh.)

A mother penguin
swims to
a snowy island.
She spent many months
in the ocean.
Her winter trip is over.

She walks to her nest.

It is made of small rocks.

Her mate has been waiting

for her there.

The place
where penguins live
is called a colony.

There are seventeen different kinds of penguins. Some live far away in hot weather. Mother and her mate are chinstrap penguins.

She and her mate will
try to have chicks.
"Hi ha hi haha!" they sing.

It is very hard
to raise two chicks.
Can they do it?

Everyone loves penguins!
What type of animal
is a penguin?

Penguins swim in the sea.

Are penguins fish?

No! They are birds!

But they cannot fly.

They do not have wings.

Penguins have flippers!

They use their flippers
to dive and swim.

Penguins dive
to catch their food.
They eat fish and krill.

Krill are like shrimp.

They swim in the ocean.

Penguins swallow

many of them at once.

Penguins walk with
two short legs.
They have their chicks
on land.

After a few weeks,
Mother lays two eggs.

Next, Father takes over.

He warms the eggs

under his body.

Mother is hungry.
She goes to the ocean
with her female friends.
They look for krill.

About ten days later,

she returns to the nest.

It is now her turn

to sit on the eggs.

The chicks are growing inside the eggs. They stay in the eggs for thirty-five days or so.

The chicks
are ready to hatch!

They break open the eggs
from inside.
They beg for food.

Both chicks
are under Mother.
Watch out! A skua!
The scary bird tries
to grab a chick.

Does she steal a chick?

No!

Mother shoos her away.

Mother and Father take turns watching the chicks. For thirty days one parent always stays with them.

The chicks cannot swim.

They are growing taller
and heavier.

But they cannot catch
the food they need.

Now both parents swim
to find them more food.
The chicks stay
with their friends.

Their parents
feed them every day.
The chicks grow fast.
Their fluffy
down feathers
will fall out.
Then they will
grow feathers
like their parents'.

Today is a big day!
The chicks enter the sea.
Now they will find
their own food.

Mother and Father
say goodbye
to each other for now.
They did it!
They were able to raise
two strong chicks.

The chicks will swim
in the ocean
for almost a year.
Then they will return
to the same colony.
See you next year,
penguins!